TITLE IX ROCKS!
PLAY LIKE A GIRL™

FAST-PITCH SOFTBALL
GIRLS ROCKING IT

ABIGAEL MCINTYRE and ANN WESLEY

rosen publishing's
rosen
central®

New York

Published in 2016 by The Rosen Publishing Group, Inc.

29 East 21st Street, New York, NY 10010

Library of Congress Cataloging-in-Publication Data

McIntyre, Abigael.
Fast-Pitch softball : girls rocking it / Abigael McIntyre and Ann Wesley.
— First Edition.
    pages cm. — ((Title IX Rocks! Play Like a Girl))
Includes index.
Audience: Grades: 7–12.
ISBN 978-1-4994-6241-8 (Library bound)
1. Softball for women—Juvenile literature. 2. Pitching (Softball)—Juvenile
literature. I. Wesley, Ann. II. Title.
GV881.3.M34 2016
796.357082—dc23

2015020130

Manufactured in China

CONTENTS

INTRODUCTION

As the batter steps up and the pitcher pauses before her throw, both girls are thinking the same thing: "I want to win." Who doesn't want to win? One of the best feelings in the world is to know you've done your best.

At first, softball was considered just that: soft. In 1887 the first softball game was played, but instead of a ball and bat, men threw a boxing glove and hit it with a stick. But this stick and glove method caught on and was developed by locals. By the 1930s, softball had become more structured and was even coordinated with the Chicago World's Fair in 1933. Numerous teams joined in the fun with fastball, slowball, and women's divisions. They played a pretty gentle game with a ball that was 14 inches (almost 36 centimeters) in diameter.

In the 1930s, baseball was not allowed at women's high schools and colleges because it was thought to be too physically difficult for them. Softball was considered a more ladylike game for them. But soon women figured out how to push the boundaries and show they could easily handle a more competitive game. By the 1940s, they were playing in leagues across the United States and even in an international game.

When younger girls were banned from baseball's Little Leagues, they tried out softball. Finally, thanks to a 1972 law that gives girls equal sports opportunities as boys in

Natasha Watley pitches for the U.S. Olympic team against Australia in the 2004 Summer Olympic Games held in Athens, Greece.

federally funded schools, known as Title IX, girls started to benefit from additional support for high school and college sports programs. Softball's competitive side was better able to flourish. Ten years later, the first Women's College World Series, which is now the national college championship for softball, was held by the National Collegiate Athletic Association (NCAA).

For some girls, softball is a chance to be rough and tough. The game is gritty—a game that gets them in the dirt and sweating, as they hit and dive for balls, then run, slide, and dive for bags (or bases) to score the next run. Sometimes they come off the field bloody, bruised, and blistered. It's not a soft game at all!

One of the great things about softball is the sheer number of playing opportunities available. As long as you can get out on the field—age two to well past retirement—you can play! No matter where you live, from the most urban city to the most rural country, there is probably a softball league to join. Organized leagues are everywhere, and they are at every level, from community and school teams straight through to college, amateur, Olympic, and professional.

Get ready to learn all about the basic game rules and how much fun it can be for anyone who plays. This resource also offers ideas for options for anyone who really wants to pursue softball and seriously stay in the game.

CHAPTER ONE

A SPORT FOR ONE, A SPORT FOR ALL

Sometimes girls don't give certain sports a try. Maybe they feel like they won't do very well if they aren't tall, thin, or athletic. Other times the best players in the game have been training practically since they could walk! This is the beauty of softball. It offers a place for just about anyone.

"Anyone with good hand-eye coordination can play," says John Carroll, the CEO of the Women's Professional Softball League. "You don't have to be six feet six. In this game you don't have to be big to play. This game appeals to a broader base of participation."

Many of the top softball players don't fit a traditional athletic body type. Players can be short, tall, average, slim, or even solid and still be good. In fact, for some positions, such as catcher, a bigger, sturdier body can be an advantage. (When a runner is sliding in to home plate and needs to get past a crouching catcher

Lisa Fernandez is living proof that all kinds of people can succeed at fast-pitch. She was told her arms were too short, but she proved otherwise.

sometimes a bigger body enables the catcher to hold her ground more easily.) In this game, a desire to win and willingness to work hard are often bigger assets than weight or height.

Lisa Fernandez, considered one of the best pitchers ever in fast-pitch softball, stands only five feet six and has an average build. Fernandez was once told she couldn't play softball because her arms were too short. But her desire to play and commitment to hard work helped her become not only one of the best college players, but also one of the best international players ever.

Softball can also be learned relatively quickly, though it may take years of practice to reach the top levels. The 2000 College World Series is a perfect example of that. Several of the players on the Southern Mississippi University (SMU) team didn't even play

THE DIFFERENCE IN PITCH

In slow-pitch softball, the ball is pitched underhand without much speed and is easy to hit. The game's focus is primarily offense and scores often run into the teens. Because most balls are hit into play, the game includes ten defensive players instead of the nine found in fast-pitch softball. Slow-pitch softball is primarily a recreational sport played in community leagues. Base stealing is not allowed, nor is bunting.

fast-pitch softball until they reached college. The basic athleticism of the players enabled them to pick up the game quickly and play on an elite level.

PLAY BALL!

Most players begin learning the game in slow-pitch leagues to master fielding, hitting, and base running, and then advance to fast-pitch leagues when they become more serious about the sport. Fast-pitch softball involves more strategy, including a variety of pitches, base stealing, and bunting.

The basic rules of fast-pitch softball are very similar to baseball. The game is divided into innings in which each team has one offensive and one defensive cycle. Each part of the cycle consists of three outs. Some of the major differences between fast-pitch softball and baseball are as follows:

- A softball game is seven innings long, and a baseball game consists of nine innings.

- Softball is played on a dirt infield, and baseball has a grass infield. The surface of the infield can affect how the ball moves.
- Softball has a flat pitching mound and baseball has a raised mound. In softball the pitch is delivered underhand while baseball involves an overhand throw.
- The softball is 11 inches (about 28 cm) in circumference in most leagues.

Softball is usually played on a dirt infield. For the Beijing 2008 Summer Games, China built the Fengtai Softball Field.

- The distance from home plate to the pitcher's mound is shorter in softball. The pitcher stands 43 feet (about 13 meters) from home plate in softball. In baseball, the pitcher is 60 feet 6 inches (about 18 m 15 cm) from the plate. However, the speed at which the ball arrives at home plate can at times be faster and thus harder to hit in softball than in baseball. While high school pitchers may hurl at 50 to 60 miles per hour (about 80 to 97 kilometers per hour), the top pitchers in the professional leagues can pitch at 70 mph (about 113 kph) or more. With the shorter distance to the plate, many compare that pitch to baseball's fastball moving at 90 to 100 mph (about 145 to 161 kph).

ESSENTIAL SOFTBALL EQUIPMENT

To begin playing softball, there is some basic equipment each girl will need. With the growth of the game, many top companies are making softball equipment specifically for girls and some national players, such as Jennie Finch, even endorse specific lines named after them. First there is the ball, and though each girl may have her own for private practice, it isn't necessary. Often a team will share several bats, but as a girl advances in the game, she may want her own bat. Each player will need her own glove. Some girls prefer to wear a batting glove, but one isn't required. Baseball or softball cleats are needed and are available at most athletic shoe stores. Catchers will need additional safety equipment. When batting, a player

Some bats are heavier and give the batter more power, but she needs the strength to move that extra weight with enough speed.

will need to wear a batting helmet, but the team generally provides several that are shared.

Bats

To judge your proper bat length, stand in place and put the bat next to you with the barrel end on the floor. If the handle hits just at your wrist, it is the correct length. If the handle is at your palm, fingers, or lower, it will be too short. If it extends up your arm, it will be too long. Finding the correct weight is a matter of personal preference and ability. Hitters have more power with a heavier bat, but only if they have the strength to swing the bat with balance and appropriate speed. The advantage of owning your own bat is that you can practice your swing during your free time and become a better hitter.

Gloves

Each player on defense will need a glove, or mitt, to catch the ball. Catchers use a special, thicker glove designed as a target and constructed to allow girls to catch balls thrown hard and fast. Outfielders tend to prefer gloves with large, long fingers that allow them to capture balls more easily, while infielders prefer gloves with shorter fingers that allow them to remove and throw the ball faster. The glove should fit comfortably and not be too large for the girl's hand.

The fast-pitch catcher is in the line of balls that can reach speeds of more than 70 mph (113 kph), so she needs the most protective gear.

Catching Equipment

The catcher needs the most equipment in order to protect herself from hard-thrown balls that may get away from her. A catcher should wear a well-fitted mask along with a throat protector, a helmet, a chest protector, and shin guards. She should make sure to wear this equipment at all times when she is behind the plate.

FROM INFIELD TO OUTFIELD: SOFTBALL POSITIONS

After the proper equipment is purchased and broken in, and the basics of the game are understood, it's time to play. While softball is easy to understand, mastering the skills needed to play well takes time and practice.

The speed of the game requires that players have quick reflexes, especially the players in the infield, who are going to have fast pitches hit directly toward them. There are six defensive positions in the infield: the pitcher and catcher who make up what is called the battery, first base, second base, shortstop, and third base. In the outfield there are three players: a left fielder, a center fielder, and a right fielder.

Pitcher and Catcher

Players interested in being a pitcher or catcher need to have good endurance because they are involved in every defensive play and also take turns at bat on offense. In addition to being strong athletes, these two players need an extra degree of mental toughness. If the pitcher walks a player or throws a bad pitch, she can't afford to get rattled or upset.

That can result in more bad pitches. She must have the ability to keep her focus on every throw. The catcher must lead the infield. Infielders face the catcher during the game, and the team takes direction from her. She must make sure everyone knows what to expect on each play, and she must keep her pitcher focused.

The pitcher has to keep her complete focus on every pitch, so she needs to be mentally and physically strong.

The pitcher generally dictates the game. A strong pitcher can stop a good hitter. The fewer times the ball is hit, the fewer chances the opponent has to score. If the pitcher is getting the ball in the strike zone and throwing hitters out, the opponent goes down fast. A good pitcher, controlling the other team, can give her teammates confidence and make them more secure at bat, knowing the other team will have a hard time scoring. A player who can handle or enjoys pressure and controlling the game makes a good pitcher.

Pitcher Lisa Fernandez often stresses the importance of brain-power over athleticism. "I'm not exceptionally fast or overly powerful. I make up for it by using technique and trying to be smarter." Complementing the pitcher is the catcher, the team leader. The catcher will get dirty and can get knocked down on plays but she must remain composed at all times. She is responsible for vocally commanding the team throughout the game. She must have very good hand-eye coordination, be flexible, and have an arm strong and accurate enough to throw from behind the plate to any of the bases. To an extent, the catcher must know every infielder's responsibility and be ready to yell it out as the ball is put in play. She must keep the team informed of how many outs there are and what the count is on each play, and she must guide the pitcher on every throw. The catcher generally sends signals to the pitcher dictating what type of pitch to throw. She must watch base runners and try to throw them out when a steal is attempted. She also calls the action on a bunt. All of this is in addition to catching every pitch and guarding home plate to prevent runners from scoring.

Catchers have to be outgoing and assertive. They can't be shy about telling other people what to do. Learning to speak up and take control is sometimes the hardest aspect of being a good catcher.

Basemen and Shortstop

The remaining infield players must have good reflexes. They must catch fast-moving balls, tag bases, and throw the ball to another fielder.

The girl playing first base is often among the tallest players on the team. She needs to provide a big target for other infielders to throw to. She also must be able to keep a foot on first base and stretch her body as far as possible toward the other bases when receiving a throw. This person must possess excellent catching skills and be reliable. All the other infielders will be throwing the ball to first base regularly. Often the balls are thrown so quickly they may not be perfectly accurate. A good athlete at first base will find ways to grab bad throws and make the outs. Her ability to get the out at first base stops any possibility of runners moving into scoring position.

Girls playing second base and shortstop are known as middle infielders. Generally, they are the most agile players on the team because they have to cover and control the largest portion of the infield. The person playing second stands a few feet from the base on the first base side. The shortstop stands between second base and third base. These two players are called on to cover their positions, make double plays, stop steals, and serve as the cutoff for outfielders throwing the ball. Quick reflexes are very important for second base and shortstop. When the ball is hit between first and second base, the girl playing second base gets the ball and the shortstop moves over to cover the base. When the ball is hit between second and third, the girl playing shortstop gets the ball and the girl playing second covers the base. The shortstop may also have to move to cover third base, if that fielder moves in to field a bunt or moves out to catch a fly ball.

Third base is often called the hot spot or hot corner. Balls reach this position very fast and the defensive player has little time to react. She must be able to snag these hits out of the air and be equally able to charge the plate to pick up a bunt and fire it to first base. This player should be someone who is aggressive, smart, and fast.

Outfield

Beyond the infield, the left, center, and right fielders are responsible for catching fly balls, picking up grounders, and getting the ball back to the infield as quickly and accurately as possible. They must make good judgments when the ball is hit, deciding in a split second where the ball is going so they can quickly move to catch it. Fielders must back each other up and communicate well to avoid colliding or letting the ball drop between them when two players are moving toward the same ball and looking up rather than at each other. Outfielders have more time to react to the ball than infielders, but unless the ball is hit exactly to them, they must move quickly to get to it and make the out. Once the ball is caught, the fielder must get it to the infield quickly to make a double play or stop runners from advancing.

BATTER UP! OFFENSE

On offense, all nine defensive players may bat or a designated hitter may bat for one offensive player. Each team establishes a batting order before the game starts and follows it throughout the game.

As with fielding, quick reflexes are essential in hitting. With balls moving toward the plate at 50 to 70 mph (about 80 to 113 kph), the hitter has no more than a second to eye it, decide where it is going, move the bat into position, and swing to send the ball back onto the field. Hitting can be the most difficult act in the sport, but it is often the most fun and popular. Being a top hitter takes an extraordinary amount of practice and work. When a batter steps in the box (the area on the right or left side of the plate measuring 3 feet wide by 7 feet long [.9 m by 2.1 m]) she must be ready to hit. Good hitters possess as many different options of moving the ball as a good pitcher. Often the coach will tell a player how or where to try to place the ball before she hits to move players already on the bases. The hitter and pitcher face off in the ultimate duel. When the hitter wins, she or a teammate safely reaches base. When the pitcher wins, they do not. While home runs are the glory hits in softball, they aren't the goal of each turn at bat. It is important to have runners on the bases to score more runs.

Sometimes, a hitter is asked to stand in the batter's box and not swing the bat. If a pitcher is struggling to get the ball in the strike

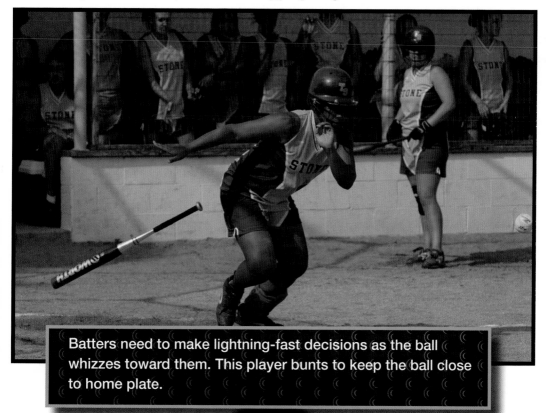

Batters need to make lightning-fast decisions as the ball whizzes toward them. This player bunts to keep the ball close to home plate.

zone, the coach will tell the hitter to hold off swinging and try to draw a walk. Knowing when the pitch is not going to be in the strike zone can be as valuable as being a home-run slugger. Getting on base gives your team more opportunities to score and puts more pressure on the defensive team because they then have to work to get the next batter out and keep you from advancing. Other times, batters may be asked to sacrifice, or put the ball into play in an area that is likely to lead to an out. The defense will often get the batter out but another base runner will have the opportunity to score or advance toward scoring. Fly balls to the outfield are often sacrifice hits, allowing a fast runner to advance from one base to the next after the ball is caught but before it is thrown back to the infield. Bunting, a short hit that moves only a few feet from home plate, is also often a way to sacrifice, although a good bunt by a fast runner can often lead to the batter and base runner advancing safely.

Of all the equipment a girl has when she gets ready to play fast-pitch softball, confidence is by far the most important. She has to step up to bat knowing she can hit the ball, regardless of who is on the pitcher's mound. It's only natural for a batter to question her talents if she has a string of unsuccessful attempts to hit. And when the pitcher stands on the mound teasing her, her confidence can plummet. But if she concentrates on nothing but the pitch when she's at bat, she increases her chances of hitting. Whether she's on the field, in the dugout, or even out in the world, the key to success is confidence.

CHAPTER TWO

GAME PREP: SKILLS AND TRAINING

Every player has a position she wants to play most—a position in which she feels completely comfortable and has the most confidence in her skills. But plenty of players learn how to play a few different positions effectively. There are a few common plays every player should know how to handle, such as fly balls and infield catches.

HOW TO CATCH FLY BALLS

Sometimes, the hardest part of catching a fly ball is judging where it will land and knowing in which direction to move to catch it. A common mistake is to start running to the ball the instant it is hit. Players should wait for just enough time to pass to determine if the ball is going to come down in front of or behind them. Moving too

The correct way to catch a fly ball is with arms and glove stretched upward with the fingers of the glove pointing up. The glove faces away from the player.

soon in the wrong direction causes the player to have to make up too much distance to get to the ball and often results in missing the catch. When the player knows in which direction to move to make the catch, it is important that she maintain eye contact with the ball and call out her intent to catch it to other players. This will prevent collisions between two players going for the same ball.

When making the fly ball catch, the ball should come down just in front of you. Catch the ball with your arms and glove extended up—the fingers of the glove should be pointing upward and the palm of the glove facing away from you. When the ball is in the glove, bring the glove down and in toward the chest to keep from dropping the ball. If runners are on base, you should then throw as fast and accurately as possible to the appropriate base or to your cutoff, a fielder who will relay the ball to the proper base. When a ball is caught deep in the outfield, another player accepts the throw halfway to the base and relays it on. She is the cutoff. When making a throw, it is important to keep the ball level or low. High arching throws from the outfield to the infield waste time.

If a short fly is hit and you are running forward from the outfield to catch it, you will change the position of the glove to catch the ball below your waist. In these cases, the glove should be turned over with the back facing the ground and the palm facing up. You should guide the ball in with your throwing hand and then quickly remove it to throw the ball to the infield. The same action should be taken for grounders coming into the outfield. Use both hands to catch the ball and bring it safely into the glove.

The best way to learn to catch fly balls is practice. One of the most common drills for learning this skill is to position girls in the outfield and have a coach hit fly balls to them, calling out the name of the girl responsible for catching each ball. Frequently during practice, one coach will work with infielders and another will use the outfield space to hit fly balls. When the full team is not practicing, two players can work together on catching fly balls by standing far apart and throwing high balls to each other.

INFIELD CATCHES

Infielders must know how to catch fly balls but must also catch a variety of other hits and must react more quickly to cover their base or catch and throw a runner out on another base. Infielders must work on receiving balls without bobbling them and must know how to throw quickly and accurately. Quick reflexes are essential. In addition to fly balls, some hitters will send the ball back as a line drive—a ball hit between waist and head height. Infielders must field line drives, as well as ground balls and bunts.

When catching a ground ball, the fielder should lower the whole glove to the ground. The body should be positioned in front of the ball, and the player should move low to it. Standing with feet apart and bending only at the waist can sometimes result in the embarrassing situation of having the ball roll through the legs. As with any catch, watch the ball all the way into the glove. The player should only move toward the rolling grounder if it is a slow roller or a bunt. Otherwise, leading the play with the glove down should give plenty of time to scoop the ball up and throw it to the appropriate base. What's important to remember is that even if the ball is dropped, if a player maintains composure, it can be quickly retrieved and the out can often still be made.

The more times girls catch and throw balls, the more comfortable they will become with fielding. The most basic and common drill begins with girls standing several feet apart throwing the ball to each other. After several successful catches they each back up and throw the ball harder and farther. As the drill continues, girls can throw different types of balls to practice different fielding techniques—grounders, high flies, pop-ups, etc. This is continued until the ball is being thrown the distance of bases. The drill allows girls to warm up before games and can help prevent arm injuries.

A STRATEGIC HIT: THE BUNT

One play every girl in fast-pitch softball must learn is the bunt. The bunt is one of the most strategic hits. It consists of the batter slapping or tapping the ball down so that it moves only a few feet from home plate. Any time there is a runner on base and zero or one out, a bunt can be expected. It is used to move the runner to the next

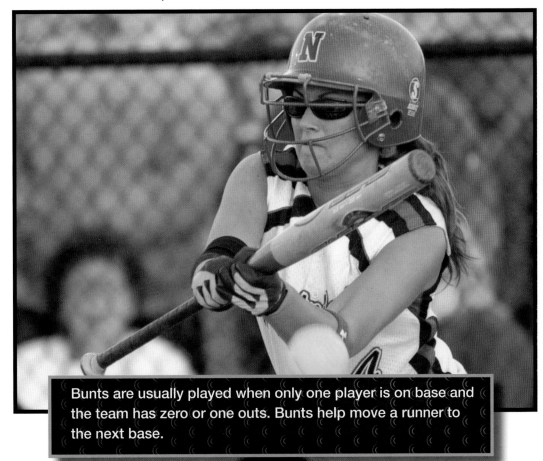

Bunts are usually played when only one player is on base and the team has zero or one outs. Bunts help move a runner to the next base.

base. Infielders generally will know when a batter is going to bunt by the way she holds the bat. Rather than holding it at the knob end with the bat barrel above the shoulders, a bunter will put one hand on the grip and the other on the barrel and hold it across her body so she can push it at a pitch.

When a bunt is shown, the fielders at first and third base should move in about halfway to the plate, close to the foul line. The second baseman will need to cover first base and the shortstop will cover second or third base depending on where the runners are and which player rushes in to field the bunt. The catcher will be the leader in fielding the bunt but the pitcher should be prepared to rush in as well. When the bunt is hit in fair territory, the catcher will play it if it is within reach. If it is hit or rolls a bit farther, the catcher will direct the play by calling out which base the fielder should throw to.

As with every aspect of softball, it takes a lot of practice to learn to hit and defend the bunt. Early on, coaches can begin by positioning the fielders and hitting bunt after bunt to show the girls the movement of the bat. Later, runners can be positioned on bases and the coach can hit bunts and allow fielders to play the ball. A considerable amount of time should be spent at each practice learning to defend against the bunt.

THE CHALLENGES OF PITCHING

For fielders to use their skills, the ball must be put into play during a game. That's where the pitcher comes in. A good pitcher can control the tempo of the game. A nervous pitcher or girl struggling to find her mark can start walking batters and the game can quickly get out of control.

Pitching is perhaps the most difficult position to learn and will take more practice than other positions. It is recommended that a girl learning to pitch partner with someone who has mastered the skill or work with an experienced pitching coach who can help her learn correct form and technique. While the underhand circular motion used in fast-pitch softball may seem unnatural, quite the opposite is true. Thrown correctly, the motion does not hurt and is not uncomfortable. Once a girl masters the basics, though, her work has just begun. From there, she will learn to throw a variety of different pitches at different speeds and place the pitch exactly where the hitters don't want it.

Understanding the basics of the pitch will help a pitcher get started. Then, as with every position, it's on to hours on the practice field. In fast-pitch softball, the pitcher holds the ball with her fingers, not in the palm of her hand. The grip on the ball should be with two or three fingers and should be firm but not too tight. When making the pitch, the arm should be relaxed through the circular motion and then snap or act like a whip to throw the pitch, with the pitcher striving for strong acceleration as the arm moves through the downward motion of the arch. As the ball is released, the pitcher will step with the pitch, but she must be sure not to lunge. The step should be made straight toward the plate. With the step, the weight must be kept back until the wrist snaps and the pitch is released. At that point, all power is thrust forward. It is important to remember that the whole body is used in the "windmill" pitch. The pitch is delivered in one motion. The ball is released when the arm comes down to the hip. The wrist snaps and the ball is hurled off the fingers toward the plate.

When learning to pitch, girls should first spend time practicing the motion and step without the ball. When they become comfortable with the circle, they can add the ball and practice the snap. Practicing the motion in front of a mirror (without throwing the ball) is a good way for a girl to see her mechanics. After the motion is

In fast-pitch softball, the player doesn't hold the ball in her palm. She holds it in a firm grip with two or three fingers.

learned, pitchers can practice against a backstop marked with a strike zone or a pitching net. Finally, after a girl learns to put the ball across the plate on a regular basis, she can begin work with a catcher and start learning to throw pitches at different angles, with different degrees of spin, speed, and placement. Meredith Shackleford, a high school pitcher who went undefeated her freshman and sophomore years, says, "I have played almost every position and the outfield. I think that every position has its difficulties. The hardest for me has always been pitching. It is the one I have put the most work into and until recently have never been satisfied with my performance. I still have a lot of work to do and will continue to work hard."

BATTER UP!

If pitching is the hardest softball skill to master, hitting is second. And everyone takes a turn at bat. Like every other skill, good hitting takes practice. A girl who owns her own bat can spend much more time practicing, learning her grip, and becoming comfortable with her swing. A girl can practice her swing just about anywhere—as long as it's a place where she doesn't have to worry about breaking anything!

The process of hitting begins with the correct grip. Your hands should be positioned close together and generally within 3 inches (7.6 cm) from the knob of the bat. The exact placement on the grip depends on each person's comfort level. The fingers should be relaxed when holding the bat—they will tighten automatically when the swing begins. The batter should stand with her feet shoulder-width apart. The knees should be slightly bent, and the weight should be on the balls of the feet. Spectators will often see batters spend a considerable amount of time kicking dirt in the batter's

When it's time to step up to the plate, the batter should keep her hands close together and close to the bat's knob.

box. This is how a batter makes sure the dirt is even under her feet. Where a girl stands in the batter's box may vary but generally, batters line their back foot up with the back of home plate.

Wherever you stand, the important thing is to make sure you are able to extend the bat over the entire plate. You should be far enough away from the plate to hit a pitch on the inside and close enough to hit the outside pitches when your arms are extended. Batters should hold the bat just off their shoulders with the arms relaxed in an upside down "V." When the pitch comes in, the batter must keep constant eye contact with the ball and stride into it as it

STEP UP TO THE T

Many players at all levels use a hitting T to practice their swing. A hitting T is a stand that the ball sits on. It enables the batter to focus on her swing instead of on the motion of the incoming ball. This allows her to hit the ball from a stationery position and focus on body movement. The direction the ball moves will quickly show errors in stance and swing. For example, if the ball is popping straight up, the player is likely dropping her shoulder and swinging up. If a girl is hitting balls that fall directly to the ground and roll, she is probably rolling her wrists rather than swinging through the pitch.

is hit. The front foot and leg will rise up and step into the pitch as the bat swings over the plate. The batter does not move forward as soon as the stride begins, but rather moves with the contact. Shifting the weight too soon will result in a loss of power on the swing. The object of the swing is to keep it level so that your arms and bat form a straight line at the point of contact. The more a girl practices the swing motion all the way through, the better she will be at hitting. Practicing the swing without a ball teaches the muscles and body the motion so that in a game situation, you can focus on watching the ball instead of thinking about your hitting motion.

A common fast-pitch drill is a short game known as pepper. In the drill, one person hits with four or five fielders standing about 20 feet (6 m) away. The first fielder tosses the ball to the hitter, and she hits it with a half swing. The next fielder then tosses the ball in and it continues. The object is to get the batter to hit a series of quick tosses to develop better hand-eye coordination. The batter is required to hit ground balls back to the fielders. If she hits a fly, she is out and the players rotate positions.

The way to learn fast-pitch is simple: get out on the field. First, players learn hitting and fielding basics, then strategies can be taught, such as base running and stealing, sliding, and place hitting, as well as assorted defensive tactics. After that the game's main challenge is just as mental as it is physical. The winning team is the one with the best strategies and performance.

CHAPTER THREE

COMPETITIVE SPIRIT

All players want to win at their sport. You hope all that hard will work pay off. But none of that matters if you don't love what you're doing. It doesn't matter if you're unwinding with a casual game in the neighborhood or working up a sweat as you train for more competitive leagues.

"Have fun. Don't get so serious at such a young age. Parents and coaches are so focused on scholarships that it takes the fun out of the game. We should enjoy the game for what it is," advises Jennifer Brundage, U.S. Olympic team member and University of Michigan assistant coach.

Winning is just icing on the cake.

TEAM PLAYERS

Jennie Finch has been playing softball since she was five years old. By age eight she was pitching. When a coach told her a few years later that she would never be a championship pitcher, she was heartbroken. But with the support of her family, especially her dad, Finch went on to become a U.S. gold medalist pitcher and Women's College World Series winner. And now she has a deep love for the sport. She told *CBS News*, "Softball has given me so much in life. It's taught me the kind of person I want to be, and given me a sweet sisterhood." Even after retiring from playing professionally, Finch spread her sheer love of the game by hosting softball camps for girls all over the United States.

Dee Dee Weiman, a pitcher in the Women's Professional Softball

U.S. gold medalist pitcher and Women's College World Series winner Jennie Finch, shown here in 2008, loves the "sweet sisterhood" of playing on a team.

League and an alternate on the 1996 Olympic team, also truly loves softball. But she emphasizes that team unity and having fun with the sport are more important than being a star. "Playing in a professional league is the first real happiness I've had in softball for a long time," she said after her first season in 1997. "I play because I love it and it's fun. Playing here is not the same as college or trying to make the Olympic team, where the pressure was so intense it wasn't fun…This is a wonderful family atmosphere where everyone is involved and everyone gets along," she said.

While any team is going to have some players who are better than others, the old saying holds that there is no "I" in team. In fast-pitch softball, it takes all players to make a team successful. This is equally true when playing offense or defense. Maybe one player is a home-run hitter. But if other members of the team aren't capable of getting on base, drawing a walk, and moving around the base path, the team likely will lose. On defense, the pitcher and catcher may receive the most attention, but when the ball is put in play, it takes all fielders playing their positions well to get the outs and move the game forward.

In fast-pitch softball, all the players must work hard to make a team successful. Trina Valencia started playing the game when she was eight years old on a team her mother coached. She stayed with the sport through college.

"I just love it. I could never do an individual sport. Just being on the team and knowing that everyone is there to accomplish something together is what I like. The competition, the situations you get into and have to get out of, that makes me feel really good," she said.

Part of being on a team means playing your role and understanding that everyone contributes. Rarely will a coach tell a player, "I want you to hit a home run" when the girl steps up to bat. Instead,

Some girls start playing softball as young as eight years old. Trina Valencia and Jennie Finch are both examples of girls who got into the game early.

the players will often be told, "We need base runners. Just a hit, we need base runners." Hitters stand a much better chance of getting on base if they try to get a hit rather than trying to smash the ball out of the park. Many games are won by the team that consistently hits the ball and works as a team advancing around the bases to home plate.

Just as hitters help the team by advancing runners, fielders have to work as a unit to keep an opponent from scoring. Take the example of a pitch thrown a bit off the mark that gets by the catcher. Working as a team, the pitcher immediately rushes the plate where the catcher throws her the ball from the spot where the ball landed. By working as a unit, the pitcher is able to stop the runner at third base from scoring. Sometimes, it takes the effort of the whole team to make a play, including those sitting on the bench in the dugout. In one tournament game, a runner at first base stole second. On the next pitch, she attempted to steal third. The catcher missed the leadoff and tossed the ball back to the pitcher. Other teammates, however, were more alert, and several girls in the dugout called the play to the pitcher. She was then able to quickly throw to third just in time to have the sliding runner tagged out. Without the effort of the whole team working together, the runner would have reached third base safely.

Communication between team members on and off the field is crucial to success in softball. When a ball is hit, two or more fielders may move toward it at the same time. Without good communication, the girls will either collide and possibly get hurt, or they will both stop, assuming the other will make the play, and the ball may drop between them.

STRENGTH OF MIND

Coaches will quickly admit that the mental game is the hardest to teach and the most important element in sports. Being mentally strong means knowing where the ball should go, paying attention, working together, listening to instructions, and executing plays as taught. It means staying composed when things don't go as planned and focusing on the task at hand rather than dwelling on a missed play.

At a high school game in Indiana, after a player struck out, ending the inning for her team, she threw her helmet in the dugout, yelled, and kicked the fence before taking her position on the field.

LAURA BERG

Olympian Laura Berg is a stand-out fast-pitch player if there ever was one, but she wasn't an instant softball star. She explained in an interview on the USA Fastpitch Softball Olympians website, "I didn't play a whole lot when I first started travel ball because of my size. I wanted to quit the team but my mom wouldn't let me. She said there's a lesson to learn from this. This made me work harder so I would never sit the bench again."

Through all her years of playing center field, Berg remembers the words of a coach, who told the team "that there are only two things you can control...

USA Fastpitch Softball Olympian Laura Berg lunges to catch the ball in a game against Australia in the 2004 Olympic Games in Athens, Greece.

your attitude and your effort." Berg explained on the Liberty Mutual website, "If I can control those two things and come ready to play I'll be ready for anything that comes my way." And Berg is clearly in complete control of her attitude and effort. She is the only player to have won four Olympic medals, three of which are Olympic gold (the fourth is silver). Today she is the head coach of the Oregon State Beavers and assistant coach of the Women's National Team.

During the game the coach told the team, "I don't care if you make a mistake. Everyone is going to make mistakes. You've just got to shake them off and put the hammer down. Play to win and keep your head in the game."

On another field on a hot August day, a team was leading 2-0 in the fifth inning when the coach called time out and huddled the team together. Rather than complimenting the players for their effort, he seriously scolded them for relaxing and losing their focus—even though they were ahead. The coach told the players the pitcher was the only team member still working. He said fielders were not standing in their ready positions, they were not talking or yelling out plays, and that they seemed to be waiting and hoping for the game to end rather than doing the things that put them on top in the game. That coach, like most others, wouldn't accept a lack of effort no matter what stage the game was in.

The ability to play the game "one pitch at a time" is a true characteristic of mental toughness. In softball, the fast action may last

In the fast-paced game of fast-pitch, every player must focus on the action at hand. It can mean the difference between the winning run or the inning's last out.

ten to fifteen seconds, followed by several minutes of slowdown or inactivity. The team that can stay mentally focused during the slow time to be sharp during the action is the team that most often comes out on top.

Physical talent is great, of course. But just ask any coach if talent alone will win games. It won't. It's those teams with the mental edge that are coming out on top.

CHAPTER FOUR

A FAST-PITCH FUTURE

It doesn't matter what level of play a girl chooses. It can be a relaxed weekend league in the city or training seriously to play in college or even professional leagues. Either way, girls who play a sport such as fast-pitch have much to gain from the experience of being on a team as well as in competition.

THE BENEFITS OF SPORTS

Participating in team sports helps provide valuable lessons for coping with situations outside of sports. Athletes learn how to work as a team, how to get along with others reaching for a common goal, how to win and loose gracefully, and the value of hard work. Through participation in sports, girls learn self-discipline, build self-confidence, and develop skills to handle competitive situations.

MEREDITH SHACKLEFORD

Meredith Shackleford started playing softball at an early age after discovering the game with her father. By the time she got to high school, her skills made her one of the top players in the country in 2000. And the lessons she learned on the field have enhanced her entire life. "Through softball, I have learned to be confident in most aspects of life. Being confident has helped me in school and to make new friends," she said. "I've also learned not to put much emphasis on day-to-day things but to look at the overall picture."

These are qualities they will need as adults in dealing with friends, relationships, employers, and people in their communities.

A nationwide study by the Women's Sports Foundation indicated that athletes do better in the classroom, are more involved in school activity programs, and stay involved in the community after graduation. The study also revealed that high school athletic participation has a positive educational and social impact on many minority and female students.

OPPORTUNITIES AT LAST

The road to opportunity has been long, but now, girls from grade school to high school, college, and beyond can't imagine not being able to play simply because of their gender. "When I was very little, I got a Wiffle ball and bat for Christmas. I played with it every day. I even broke out one of our basement windows. Softball is so

Studies show that team sports have a lot to teach players, including working as a team, the value of hard work, and self-confidence.

fun. It's a dirty game and I love playing it," said Michelle McCrady, who played from childhood through high school and into college, in 2000.

McCrady and other girls have more opportunity than ever before to continue playing past high school. Since the fast-pitch

game became an official NCAA sport in 1982, the number of educational institutions sponsoring the sport has grown at a steady rate. In 1982, there were 143 Division I collegiate teams, no teams in Divisions II or III, 243 junior college teams, and 7,569 high school teams. According to the Eastern Girls Fast Pitch Softball League, by 2007 Division I had expanded to 277, with the number of youth teams also increasing to 86,049. By 2015, there were 295 Division I NCAA teams, 290 Division II, and 420 Division III.

Together, softball and baseball ranked as the third most popular high school sport for girls in 2013, surpassed only by basketball and volleyball, according to ESPN. That same year, softball attracted 17 percent of girls to play.

ON TO THE OLYMPICS

The growth of the fast-pitch game began with Title IX but continued to flourish with the success of the U.S. Olympic team in 1996—the first year the sport was in the Olympics—and 2000. Prior to the 1996 Olympics, the national team toured a half dozen U.S. cities to introduce the sport's players and build excitement for the games. When the national team and U.S. practice team played in the Midwest, thousands of fans turned out to watch the action, filling stadiums and every inch of grass behind the outfield in many cases. While many people attended out of curiosity, once fans got to see the fast-paced action, they were quickly won over.

Today, the opportunities to keep playing softball long after high school are more numerous than ever.

Perhaps the biggest compliment for the sport came when a male reporter voiced his amazement at the game. "I was impressed by the outstanding overall athleticism, and especially enamored of the pitching. I saw rising fastball after rising fastball (interspersed with the occasional knee-buckling change-up) rocketing homeward and thought to myself, 'There is no way on God's green earth I could hit that,'" he wrote.

The reaction wasn't unusual as new fans told sports leaders they wanted more. The support resulted in the Women's Pro Softball League, which now runs every summer and is televised nationally on sports networks.

Dot Richardson, an Olympian and surgeon, notes, "Even though some women play baseball, softball is still the avenue for girls who love to hold a glove and throw a ball and rip the cover off of it."

FAITH IN THE FUTURE

In 2006, fast-pitch was dealt a brutal blow. The International Olympic Committee (IOC) decided to remove both softball and baseball from the 2012 Olympic Games and then again for the 2016 games. In the summer of 2015, the possibility of fast-pitch returning to the Olympics in 2020 was still bright, but far from certain.

Meanwhile, the Amateur Softball Association (ASA) established the World Cup of Softball in Oklahoma City, where the world's top teams could still come and compete. And in 2015 the Pan American Games were still going strong, with Laura Berg and Lisa Dodd serving as two of the U.S. team's assistant coaches along with Howard Dobson and head coach Ken Eriksen. Also on the team is World Cup gold medalist pitcher Valerie Arioto. "We're excited to get out there and play tomorrow," she said on the National Fastpitch Coaches Association website. "This team is special and we just really enjoy playing together and playing hard together." And that is what the game of fast-pitch should be all about.

TIMELINE

1887 George Hancock, a reporter for the Chicago Board of Trade, develops the idea for the game of softball after watching Yale and Harvard supporters throw a boxing glove and try to hit it with a stick.

1895 The first women's softball team is formed at Chicago's West Division High School. They did not have a coach for competitive play until 1899.

1920s–1930s Softball becomes a popular sport for U.S. women as high schools and colleges promote it in female physical education courses.

1931 Baseball commissioner Kenesaw Mountain Landis bans women from professional baseball (the ban lasts until 1992), after seventeen-year-old pitcher Virne Beatrice "Jackie" Mitchell strikes out Babe Ruth and Lou Gehrig in an exhibition game for the Chattanooga Lookouts. Landis voids Mitchell's contract, saying baseball is "too strenuous" for women.

1933 The Amateur Softball Association (ASA) is founded. The group is now the strongest softball organization in the country, and with USA Softball, it governs the sport. The game officially becomes known as softball.

At the Chicago National Softball Tournament, the male and female champions are honored equally.

1943 Phillip K. Wrigley, owner of the Chicago Cubs, establishes the All-American Girls Softball League, the forerunner of the All-American Girls Baseball League.

1951 Betty Chapman becomes the first black American

professional softball player as an outfielder on the Admiral Music Maids of the National Girls Baseball League of Chicago.

1965 The first international women's softball tournament is held in Melbourne, Australia, with the home country beating the United States in the finals, 1–0.

1976 The Connecticut Falcons beat the San Jose Sunbirds in the first Women's Professional Softball World Series championship.

1972 Title IX is passed into law, requiring that women in federally funded schools receive opportunities in sports that are equal to those enjoyed by men. "No person in the United States shall, on the basis of sex, be excluded from participation in, be denied the benefits of, or be subject to discrimination under any education program or activities receiving Federal financial assistance."

1975 The International Women's Professional Softball League forms. The league disbands in 1980 because of financial problems.

Title IX officially goes into effect on June 21.

1979 Softball debuts at the Pan American Games, with the United States Women's National Team winning the gold medal.

1982 First National Collegiate Athletic Association Division I Softball Championship; UCLA defeats Fresno State 2–0 in eight innings.

Dot Richardson hits the first home run in women's Olympic softball.

1984 The U.S. women's softball squad wins the championship in the first Women's International Cup, beating China 1–0.

1996 Softball is recognized as an official Olympic sport. The United States wins gold.

1997 The first women's professional fast-pitch game is played on May 30, with the Virginia Roadsters defeating the Durham Dragons 2–1.

1999 A total of 2,445,585 adults register to play in ASA-sanctioned leagues.(cure

There are 1,245,525 players eighteen years old and under who register to play in ASA-sanctioned leagues.

2000 The United States successfully defends its gold medal at the Olympic Games.

2005 ASA creates the World Cup of Softball.

2006 International Olympic Committee (IOC) votes to remove softball and baseball from the Olympic program in 2012.

2009 The IOC upholds its decision to exclude baseball and softball for the 2016 Olympic games.

2012 On June 16, the Chicago Bandits' Monica Abbott breaks a personal record as well as a speed record for women's fast-pitch: 77 mph (about 124 kph).

GLOSSARY

AMATEUR A level of sports in which players play for enjoyment and are not paid.

AMATEUR SOFTBALL ASSOCIATION A volunteer not-for-profit organization that regulates competition in softball to make sure the sport is fair and equal for everyone who plays.

BAG The base.

BOBBLE To fumble the ball, such as by dropping it, for example.

BUNT A legally hit ball that is not swung at, but rather tapped slowly within the infield.

CHANGE-UP A straight pitch that goes over the plate at about two-thirds the speed of a fastball.

CLEAT A type of shoe worn in some sports that has many pieces of wood, rubber, or other material on the sole to help players keep their footing.

COUNT The number of balls and strikes in a softball game.

DEFENSE In sports, the team or players that are trying to prevent the other team from scoring or advancing the ball.

DESIGNATED HITTER A hitter designated to bat for any one starting player.

DOUBLE PLAY When two base runners are called out on the same play.

ELITE The people who are considered the top performers in their field because of their skill, strength, or wealth.

FASTBALL The most common pitch in softball. It is a straight pitch thrown as fast as possible with a forward rotation.

FLY BALL A ball that is hit very high into the air.

FOUL A ball batted outside of fair territory.

GROUND BALL A ball that is hit along the ground.

INFIELD Fair territory within the base paths.

INNING The segment of a game where each team has a turn at bat and in which there are three outs for each team. In softball, there are seven innings. In baseball, there are nine innings.

INTERNATIONAL WOMEN'S PROFESSIONAL SOFTBALL (IWPS) Formed in 1976, this softball league lasted only three years because of a lack of financial support.

NATIONAL COLLEGIATE ATHLETIC ASSOCIATION (NCAA) An organization run by members who make sure student players are safe, educated, and skilled on the field, in the classroom, and in life.

NATIONAL PRO FASTPITCH (NPF) First known as the Women's Pro Softball League, the NPF provides entertainment for everyone by offering games that feature the best in fast-pitch softball.

OFFENSE In sports, the team or players that are trying to score or advance the ball. Also, the team in possession of the ball.

OUTFIELD The fair territory beyond the infield.

OVERHAND A pitch or throw in which the hand moves above shoulder level and with the palm over or covering the ball.

OVERTHROW To throw above or beyond a base person's or fielder's reach.

POP-UP A short, high fly in or near the infield.

PROFESSIONAL Engaging in a sport or other activity as paid work, rather than for fun.

SACRIFICE Advancing a runner by forcing a play on the batter. For example, the batter will hit a fly ball to the outfield, knowing it will most likely be caught for an out but that it will allow the base runner to advance.

SANCTION Give authorized consent or permission for.

SHORTSTOP The infield player who stands between second base and third base. Also refers to the position on the field.

SLOW-PITCH SOFTBALL A type of softball in which the ball is pitched underhand without much speed and is easy to hit.

STEALING A base runner trying to advance to the next base as the pitcher throws the ball to the batter.

STRIKE ZONE Any area above home plate between the batter's knees and armpits when using a normal batting stance.

TITLE IX A law passed in 1972 that prohibits discrimination based on sex and gives women and men equal sports opportunities in federally funded schools.

TRAVEL BALL Softball or baseball teams that are more competitive, or "select," and travel to play games outside the home area. Players are required to try out for these teams.

UNDERHAND A pitch or throw in which the ball remains below shoulder level and with the palm of the hand facing upward or outward.

WALK When a batter has four balls called and may advance safely to first base.

WIFFLE BALL A type of baseball in which the ball is light and hollow and has holes.

WINDMILL A pitching delivery in which the pitcher's arm moves in a circle starting in front of the body, swinging over the head, and ending just after the hand and arm pass the pitcher's hips.

FOR MORE INFORMATION

Amateur Softball Association of America (ASA)

ASA/USA Softball—National Headquarters

ASA Hall of Fame Stadium Complex

2801 N.E. 50th Street

Oklahoma City, OK 73111

(405) 424-5266

Website: http://www.softball.org

The ASA, which is the national governing body of softball, is primarily responsible for providing structured leagues for nearly four million players, coaches, and umpires. The ASA establishes uniform softball rules and regulations and provides instruction in the game to both coaches and players. Visit the local contacts and websites page to find information specific to your state and city.

Canadian Open Fastpitch Society

#457, 800-15355 24th Avenue

Surrey, BC V4A 2H9

Canada

(604) 536-9287

Website: http://www.canadianopenfastpitch.com

The Canadian open Fastpitch Society is a nonprofit society "dedicated to advocating and encouraging the development of the sport of softball by staging a first class, family oriented elite international fastpitch event," the Canadian Open Fastpitch International Championship.

National Collegiate Athletic Association (NCAA)
700 W. Washington Street
P.O. Box 6222
Indianapolis, IN 46206
(317) 917-6222
Website: http://www.ncaa.org
News, standings, and information about official NCAA Division
I, II, and III collegiate softball.

National Fastpitch Coaches Association
2641 Grinstead Drive
Louisville, KY 40206
(502) 409-4600
Website: http://www.nfca.org
This organization supports coaches of all levels of fast-pitch
softball. This site features fast-pitch news and other information, such as camps, jobs, conventions, and more.

National Pro Fastpitch (NPF)
3350 Hobson Pike
Hermitage, TN 37076
Website: http://www.profastpitch.com
Official site of the NPF, with links to member teams, news, and
information.

Softball Canada
223 Colonnade Road, Suite 212
Ottawa, ON K2E 7K3
Canada
(613) 523-3386

Website: http://www.softball.ca

Founded in 1965, the Canadian Amateur Softball Association, or Softball Canada is a nonprofit organization that is considered softball's governing body.

Women's Sports Foundation (WSF)

247 West 30th Street, Suite 7R

New York, NY 10001

(800) 227-3988

(646) 845-0273

Website: http://www.WomensSportsFoundation.org

Founded by the renowned tennis champion Billie Jean King, the WSF continues its work in "advancing the lives of girls and women through sports and physical activity" with a board of trustees that includes female athletes, businesspeople, and leaders of women's sports organizations, just to name a few.

WEBSITES

Because of the changing nature of Internet links, Rosen Publishing has developed an online list of websites related to the subject of this book. This site is updated regularly. Please use this link to access the list:

http://www.rosenlinks.com/IX/Soft

FOR FURTHER READING

Babb, Ron. *Etched in Gold: The Story of America's First-Ever Olympic Gold Medal Winning Softball Team*. Indianapolis, IN: Masters Press, 1997.

Baker, Jayne. *An Insider's Guide to Softball.* New York, NY: Rosen Young Adult, 2014.

Brill, Marlene Targ. *Winning Women in Baseball and Softball.* Hauppauge, NY: Barron's, 2000.

Cook, Colleen Ryckert. *Dream Jobs in Coaching* (Great Careers in the Sports Industry). New York, NY: Rosen Publishing, 2012.

Elliott, Jill, and Martha Ewing, eds. *Youth Softball: A Complete Handbook*. Dubuque, IA: Brown and Benchmark, 1992.

Dzidrums, Christine, and Leah Rendon. *Jennie Finch: Softball Superstar* (Y Not Girl). Whittier, CA: Creative Media Publishing, 2013.

Finch, Jennie, and Ann Killion. *Throw Like a Girl: How to Dream Big and Believe in Yourself.* Chicago, IL: Triumph Books, 2011.

Garman, Judy. *Softball Skills and Drills*. Champaign, IL: Human Kinetics, 2011.

Howell, Brian. *Girls' Softball*. Minneapolis, MN: ABDO Publishing Co., 2014.

Johnson, Jeremy. *Unusual and Awesome Jobs in Sports: Pro Team Mascot, Pit Crew Member, and More* (You Get Paid for THAT?). North Mankato, MN: Capstone Press, 2015.

LaBella, Laura. *Dream Jobs in Sports Fitness and Medicine*

(Great Careers in the Sports Industry). New York, NY: Rosen Publishing, 2012.

Mattison, Bob. *The Game Is for the Girls: The Story of Golden Valley Girls Softball.* Davenport, IA: Fidlar Doubleday, 2011.

Richardson, Dot, and Don Yaeger. *Living the Dream.* New York, NY: Kensington Books, 1997.

Schwartz, Heather E. *Girls' Softball: Winning on the Diamond* (Girls Got Game). Mankato, MN: Capstone Press, 2007.

Smith, Michelle. *Coach's Guide to Game-Winning Softball Drills: Developing the Essential Skills in Every Player.* Camden, ME: McGraw-Hill, 2008.

Steidinger, Joan. *Sisterhood in Sports: How Female Athletes Collaborate and Compete.* New York, NY: Rowman & Littlefield, 2014.

Swope, Bob. *Teach'n Beginning Defensive Fast Pitch Softball Drills: Drills, Plays, Situations and Game Free Flow Handbook.* St. Louis, MO: Jacobob Press, 2014.

Trimble, Richard, and Pat Barnaba. *The Ultimate Softball Drill Book: A Complete Guide for Indoor and Outdoor Skill Development.* Baltimore, MD: PublishAmerica, 2013.

Weekly, Ralph, and Karen Weekly. *High-Scoring Softball.* Champaign, IL: Human Kinetics, 2012.

INDEX

ABOUT THE AUTHOR

Abigael McIntyre is a writer who enjoys most sports, including volleyball, softball, and field hockey, but especially those played in the great outdoors. She also enjoys hiking and backpacking in Montana's Beartooth Mountains.

Ann Wesley lives and works in Bloomington, Indiana, and is an avid sports fan. She has a degree in journalism from Indiana University and has written for newspapers and magazines. Wesley currently works as a director of a web design company.

CREDITS

Cover, pp. 44, 46–47 Jan de Wild/Shutterstock.com; p. 5 Ezra Shaw/Getty Images; p. 8 © Tampa Bay Times/ZUMA Press; pp. 10–11 MCT/Tribune News Service/Getty Images; p. 12 Andy Cross/The Denver Post/Getty Images; p. 13 © Dennis MacDonald/Alamy; p. 15 Wesley Hitt/Stone/Getty Images; pp. 19, 25, 28, 30 The Washington Post/Getty Images; pp. 22, 40–41 Portland Press Herald/Getty Images; p. 34 Al Bello/Getty Images; p. 36 Stacy Barnett/iStock/Thinkstock; p. 38 Nick Laham/Getty Images; cover and interior pages graphic elements vector illustration/Shutterstock.com.
Designer: Nicole Russo; Editor: Jacob Steinberg; Photo Researcher: Carina Finn

[5]